The Designer's Eye

VISUAL PROBLEM-SOLVING IN ARCHITECTURE

Brent C. Brolin

W · W · Norton & Company · New York · London

For information about permission to reproduce selections from this book,
write to Permissions, W. W. Norton & Company, Inc.,
500 Fifth Avenue, New York, NY 10110

The text of this book is composed in Scala Sans
with the display set in Helvetica Neue Outline
Composition by Ken Gross
Manufacturing by Courier Companies Inc.
Book design by Antonina Krass

Library of Congress Cataloging-in-Publication Data
Brolin, Brent C.
  The designer's eye: visual problem-solving in architecture / Brent C. Brolin
      p.   cm.
  ISBN 0-393-73068-9
  1. Architecture—Details. 2. Architecture—Composition, proportion, etc. 3. Visual perception. I. Title.

NA2840 .B755   2002
721—dc21   2002022742

W. W. Norton & Company, Inc., 500 Fifth Avenue,
New York, N.Y. 10110
www.wwnorton.com

W. W. Norton & Company Ltd., Castle House,
75/76 Wells Street, London W1T 3QT

 3 4 5 6 7 8 9 0

CONTENTS

INTRODUCTION

The two pictures at the right are almost identical. In the lower photograph a line cuts across the building (it's a vivid red in the original). The line has a visual impact. It emphasizes horizontality in two ways. It is like a measuring tape running across the full width of the building saying, "Look how wide I am." It is also a divider. It slices through the only element that challenges the building's horizontality, cutting the squarish block to the left of the entrance into two horizontally proportioned rectangles.

The red line is a simple visual device that has a major impact on the way viewers see the building. It is an exercise in the visual craft of design. The thesis of this book is that visual choices have visual consequences. The following pages contain more than a hundred "with" and "without" comparisons. Each pair illustrates how a designer's choice influences our perception of a building.

Architects have spun sophisticated theories to explain why their buildings look the way they do. The most familiar is the modernists' creation of functionalism—the idea that the plain forms of contemporary architecture were a simple, no-nonsense response to functional requirements. But looking closely at buildings suggests that something more basic is at the heart of why buildings look the way they do. If the forms of contemporary architecture really were based solely on function, why don't all office towers look the same? (See Figures 1 and 2.) Common sense tells us that buildings look the way they do because their designers want them to look that way. Architects have aesthetic preferences (what used to be called taste), and they make design choices based on those preferences.

Why is aesthetic preference or taste the prime determinant of appearance rather than function or some other ideological design rationalization? Because there are many different visual solutions to any architectural problem. These provide designers with a range of workable visual solutions from which to choose.

Consider the following common design problem. You are planning a room and it needs light and air. The obvious solution is to provide a window. But windows come in a staggering variety of shapes and styles and, to complicate matters, they can be arranged in many different configurations, most of which may meet a client's requirements. Enter aesthetic choice. You pick the solution that suits your aesthetic bent from the several options that meet the requirements. You make a design decision based on what your eyes tell you.

The simplest, most basic design decisions can have resounding visual consequences. Consider the tops of building. All buildings meet the sky, but they can do so in many ways. They may be chopped off flat

Fig. 1   Fig. 2

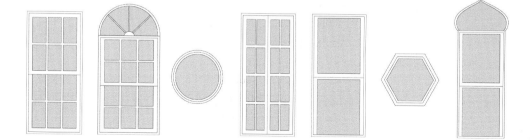

(as in the photograph at right) or drawn out to a point (as shown in the far-right photograph), with a full complement of options in between. Chopped off is not inherently better than drawn out, but each evokes a different feeling in the viewer.

Some architects may intuit the visual consequences of their choices rather than verbalize them. There is nothing wrong with that—it is the end result that counts—but there is a benefit in making choices explicit. Spelling out the visual impact of a particular preference requires you to clarify your visual intention. It suggests a heightened degree of consciousness about what you are doing. It permits you to step back, figuratively speaking, and analyze what is on the drawing board or screen. And that, in turn, encourages a comparison between visual intention and realization. If the execution does not yield the intended result, you have uncovered an inconsistency between what you expected to achieve visually and what your exercise of the craft of design actually yielded, and you can adjust accordingly. Stepping back to analyze what you have done may also reveal that there was no specific visual intention. In this case, as you will learn, your choices do have visual consequences whether you are aware of them or not. It is better to try to control these consequences; the alternative is to discover them when it is too late to change them.

Being explicit about your visual intentions also adds flexibility to the design process by pointing out possible alternatives. Noticing that a truncated top creates one kind of feeling necessarily makes you aware of alternatives—the drawn-out form, for instance.

In short, being aware of your visual intentions and their consequences can both clarify and enrich the search for design solutions.

Any interest in how buildings appear to viewers necessarily focuses on details. It is through the progression of details at different scales, revealed as we approach a building, that architects achieve subtlety and richness of expression. Buildings with a limited range of details generally do not hold our interest for long. Just what constitutes detail depends on the viewing distance. In this book I define "detail" broadly, and the term frequently overlaps with "ornament." I take into consideration changes in scale, as the four photographs at right show. When you first see the city from a distance, the spires of Chartres Cathedral are a tiny detail on the horizon, but as you near the cathedral, you are treated to details of increasingly finer scale.

Each example on the following pages consists of two pictures. The altered building always appears on the left, the actual building on the right. In the brief comments accompanying these pictures I have tried (though not always successfully) to avoid aesthetic value judgments. However, taste is of secondary importance here. I encourage readers to focus on the visual device that makes one picture different from the other, and to understand how it affects the way we see the building.

The examples were chosen because each contains something visually interesting, some element that tickled my eye. By default, this approach resulted in a wide variety of buildings, from world famous to distinctly humble. (Where the information for a building was available, the location, architect, and completion date are given at the back of the book.) Though this approach may seem haphazard, it was the natural outcome of looking for visual ideas rather than architectural pedigrees.

A word about the sidelights—the small pictures that accompany some examples. Design is a language, and the choices designers make inevitably say something to the viewer. That message may be subtle or bold, dull or electrifying. The sidelights are intended to illuminate the visual ideas contained in the main examples.

I hope this book helps architects hone their skills, and that it adds another layer of pleasure to the visual life of nonprofessionals for whom architecture is a spectator sport. If I succeed in either goal, it should result in a greater understanding and appreciation of the architect's work.

Facades

This is a great block of a building. The taper toward the top reduces its mass somewhat but emphasizes the sheer breadth of the facade.

Bowing the center panel and introducing a different color and texture make the facade seem skinnier, because the viewer sees three narrow elements rather than a single broad one.

The frieze below the eave of this country house is blank and lacks texture compared to the other elements—shingles, clapboard, even the picket fence.

A simple row of blocks creates a more sympathetic visual texture. Instead of grasping the frieze in one continuous sweep, the viewer's eye now moves from block to block. The pattern is also more in keeping with the rest of the structure.

A tall, wide building is out of place in a neighborhood of narrow townhouses (see sidelight).

The building's apparent width is reduced by running back-to-back quoins down its center, converting it into two narrow buildings.

Neighboring houses.

Diagonal bracing suggests a rigid support for the pediment above these dormer windows.

Curved scrolls still convey the feeling of support but give a more informal, relaxed appearance.

This roof seems to press down on the floors below. It is a cap or container that ends the building.

A strip of windows suggests that the roof floats above the lower floors because glass does not appear load-bearing. The glass opens up the top rather than closing it in.

An enclosing cap.

A typical skyscraper facade in the modern mode emphasizes the vertical, with secondary spandrels between the columns.

Putting the normally internal cross-bracing on the outside shows the viewer what is keeping the building stable, and physically and visually ties the facade together.

The corset ties (top) and the bands wrapping the Roman fasces (bottom) provide the same visual sense of binding together.

A two-story space (the box that breaks the roofline) interrupts the horizontal sweep of this township building.

Slicing the squarish box in two with a long line emphasizes the horizontality of the structure. The two-story box is now two long rectangles, one atop the other.

This building has two facade treatments beneath its capping top: a dark, mainly glass portion that wraps around a lighter, mainly masonry one. The glass and masonry sections are so distinct as to seem unrelated.

A light-colored grid, marking slabs and columns of the glass portion of the facade, makes a color reference to the masonry section and visually links the two elements in a more unified composition.

The brick pattern of this facade is visible from close up but is too fine to interest the eye from a distance: it becomes a blur.

Two simple devices break up the plane of the facade and provide a larger-scale texture that reads from a distance. Continuous white lintels cap the windows; punched holes and incised vertical grooves in the brick facade plane create a staccato rhythm.

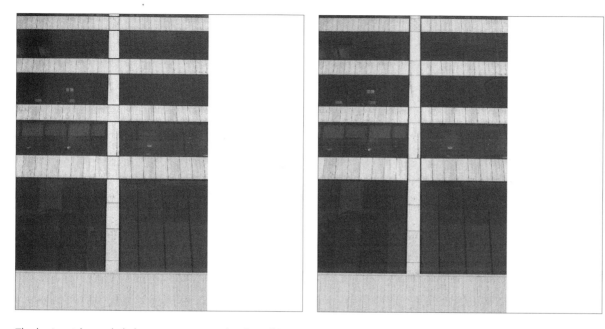

The horizontal spandrels here appear to overlay the columns, interrupting the vertical progress of the eye and emphasizing the horizontal.

Replacing the horizontal reveals, cutting across the columns, with vertical ones, cutting across the spandrels, shifts the visual right-of-way to the vertical. The column now dominates and slides by the spandrels with no suggestion of an interruption.

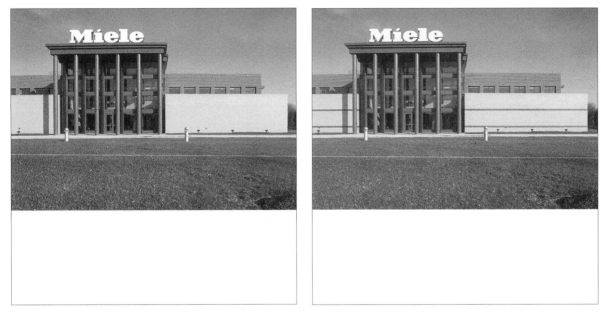

The high walls on either side of the colossal portico may enhance the grand scale of the entrance, but they compete with the portico.

Adding simple string courses of a contrasting color to the side walls slices them into horizontal sections, reducing their apparent height. They are just as tall but seem less imposing, and that makes the entrance portico appear more important.

The narrowness of this university cultural center facade accentuates the vertical attenuation of its three stories.

Horizontal moldings divide the building into a less extreme, less "straining upwards" composition.

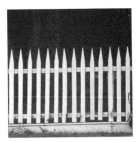

The walls of a sunken courtyard pen the viewer in. The sharp angles at the top edge are like spikes on a prison wall: we have to force our eyes over the top. The step-back helps diminish the effect, but does not dispel it.

Replace the right angles with curves and the corners are no longer hostile. The viewer's eye doesn't catch at the top, but slides over. Now we seem to be at the bottom of a gentle waterfall rather than in a prison yard.

An aggressive picket fence.

The difference between these two pictures is subtle. Here the front portion of the facade is pulled away from the rest of the building for emphasis but still seems connected to it by the white string course. The string course also creates the illusion of an "attic" story—a separate element that seems to sit on top of the main building.

Removing the string course from the entrance facade detaches it from the sides of the building and increases its apparent size. The top seems to swell in scale compared to the rest of the building, rising above the apparent top created by the string course.

Tying things together.

The connection between these side-by-side doors is ambiguous —are they related or not?

An unobtrusive but critical dividing line, the downspout placed between the doors separates them decisively.

The windows of this apartment house, in apparently random sizes, line up vertically but give little sense of horizontal continuity.

Emphasizing the horizontal connection of the openings with brick creates horizontal bands defining each floor.

A strong linear band isolates the layers of windows.

The windows and doorways on the tower and side of this cathedral are functional, but hardly celebratory.

Simple white outlines increase the apparent size of the openings, especially the round windows, and suggest a more formal composition, like white tie and tails. The horizontal moldings on the tower create the impression of a much more substantial crown. The pediment and frame around the entrance bolster its importance.

The eye moves up this tower in a single, unimpeded sweep.

Using stacked units to compose the tower makes it seem less vertical. The viewer's eye pauses at each cornice.

The composition of a famous Florentine tower also distracts from the vertical.

In tacit acknowledgment of this stunningly awkward relationship between old and new, the architect made the tower surface reflective, perhaps hoping that would make it recede somewhat.

Carving a V into the tower facade makes it less overpowering because it reads as two narrower facades rather than one broad one.

This baroque church facade with its huge entablature is a looming presence in a monumental piazza.

Moving the entablature down from the top reduces the apparent height of the facade because the viewer sees the entablature as the top, and the newly created attic story above as an element that is "added on."

This tall building is out of scale with the smaller houses (seen left and right) and civic buildings that share the town square.

Changing the direction of the moldings cuts the gable into a series of horizontal forms, reducing its apparent height and helping make it more sympathetic to its neighbors.

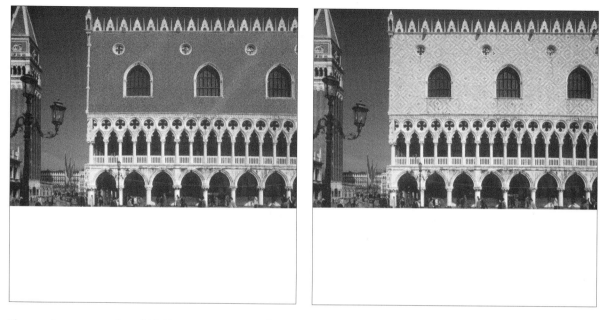

The massive upper portion of this Venetian Renaissance facade overpowers the delicate arcades below.

Patterns, particularly nondirectional ones, distract from mass. The eye becomes intrigued with their intricacies and the viewer forgets the solidity of the walls on which the patterns sit.

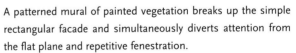

A conventionally bland apartment facade.

A patterned mural of painted vegetation breaks up the simple rectangular facade and simultaneously diverts attention from the flat plane and repetitive fenestration.

Detail of the mural (top). Ornamental hinges on the door of a French Romanesque church similarly distract from the plane of the door (bottom).

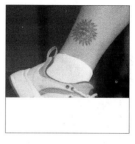

An urban nightmare: a few thousand square feet of blank, concrete wall present nothing to interest the eye.

A single painted figure creates a focal point that grabs the eye and diverts attention from the naked facade.

The ankle tattoo is also intended to attract the eye.

This south German house is a great block, like a broad Bavarian hausfrau.

A girdle of tile diverts attention from the bulk of the house, encouraging us to see its three elements, bottom, middle and top, rather than one chunky volume.

Another way to divide one large element.

This building looks its four-story height.

The same building looks lower and less massive when the two top floors are painted a different, lighter color, breaking the composition into a lower and an upper layer instead of one solid block.

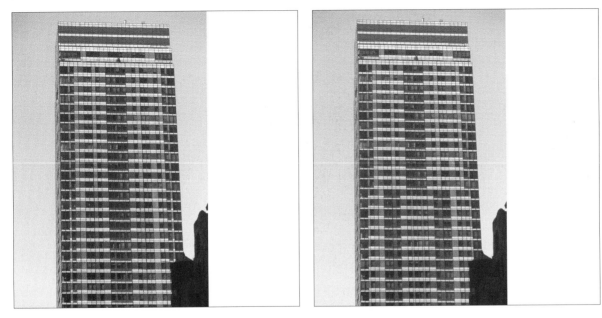

Only the rudimentary horizontal cap at the top mitigates the repetitiveness of this modern apartment facade.

The judicious grouping of similar elements creates patterns that break up the facade into smaller, more varied groupings.

The blank side of this skyscraper closes off the building; it frames and contains it.

Cutting a huge slot in the side suggests a lighter structure and gives a generally more open feeling.

The shallow reveals and finely scaled details of this curved facade suggest a graceful, thin surface.

The sense of thinness can actually be heightened by adding thickness. Push the plane of the windows out a few inches, and "fasten" them to the resulting frame (using ornamental elements that read like "clips"), and a skin of windows appears to have been stretched over the curved frame of the facade, like a sail filled by the wind.

Detail of clip connection.

The bend in the middle distracts somewhat from the great width of this dormitory building.

Still the same width, the building seems less wide when the contrasting panel inserted in the center breaks it into three separate sections, the two outer ones embracing the central one.

Contemporary and traditional variations on same idea—breaking up mass.

A slick shop entrance blends in with the shopscape left and right.

Gouging out a striking artificial fissure above the entrance, complete with severed pipes ready to spew forth their contents, has an obvious shock effect; you don't expect cracks in construction. The faux fissure also increases the apparent size of the entrance, much as a swan's neck pediment does in more traditional design.

Detail of entrance (top). Swan's neck pediment (bottom).

This broad, elegantly proportioned facade actually spans two houses.

The single volume becomes two, and the proportion of the facade changes, when color breaks up the block.

There is a discontinuity between the top and midsection of this building. The relatively shallow upper story sits on top like a beanie on a middle linebacker.

When the color of the top story is brought down into the midsection, it creates a visual link between the two, and reduces the apparent area of the facade of the lower floors.

Out-of-scale beanie (top). Repeating shades of tie and hankie connect the elements of this sartorial ensemble (bottom).

We are very much aware of the solid, weblike surface of the abutments between these arches.

Punching holes in the abutments makes us focus on the holes—the space—rather than the solids. When we can see through something, we perceive it as lighter rather than heavier.

Perforations lighten masonry wall.

This apartment house has a nearly neutral, nondirectional window pattern.

Adding panels of stacked radial brick between the windows links the windows on each floor. Though the radial bricks are obviously different from the windows to the left and right, the combination creates an element that contrasts with the plain-bond brick texture above and below to create a facade of horizontal layers.

Introducing a pier does not disrupt the rhythm of this colonnade.

This huge commercial block has no particular visual focus.

Adding towers begins to suggest a rhythm, but the building remains a massive block. Darkening certain sections makes them recede and suggests, rather audaciously, that they aren't actually there. The illusion of stepped towers yields a bold, swinging cadence that is so convincing it seems about to produce a third tower at the left.

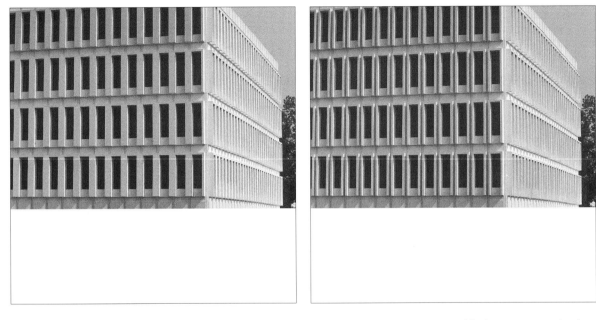

Heavy, vertical mullions separate the windows on a squat, massive office building.

These mullions are the same width, but grooves make them appear lighter.

This tall slab of concrete wants to be a tower but its unrelieved blockiness ties it to the ground.

An incised pattern of vertical lines reduces the apparent mass and divides the block into a series of long, tall panels that emphasize the vertical.

Vertical emphasis.

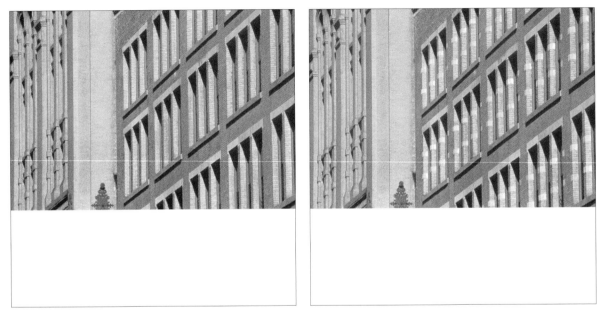

The windows of this facade are quite tall and narrow.

Two bands of lighter stone cutting across the frames divide the tall windows into three shorter, stacked segments. They are still tall but the viewer's eye connects the dots into horizontal lines that subdivide the openings and distract from their height.

Horizontal moldings break up verticality of the tower.

This elaborate entrance to an entertainment center is staid and bland.

Add two round windows and the character—or one might say expression—of the facade changes completely. Now it's a face, and a rather startled one at that.

Anthropomorphic chimney pots.

A simple, unembellished adobe building.

The darker, painted base gives the facade more visual weight; the building acquires stature. The stripe above the base creates a visual/mechanical link that binds the top and bottom sections together. Without it (see left illustration) the upper and lower sections are less firmly connected. Reversing the colors would put the visual weight on top (see upper sidelight).

Dark color above puts the visually "heavy" element on top (top). "Grabbing" with fingers rather than lines (bottom).

The rather wide facade on this university administration building has no particular focus. It just starts at one end and ends at the other, with little of interest going on in between.

The grand semicircular pediment provides a central flourish. Alone, it might be out of place—too small for the width—but the two sibling pediments left and right make a composition that builds toward the center. The slit skylight in the center of the roof acts as an exclamation point over the main pediment, and also breaks up the very long stretch of roof.

Repetitive balconies in textured concrete are unrelieved and make this apartment building seem quite dense and heavy.

Perforating the solid railings lightens the facade while retaining the sense of massiveness.

Part of a huge exhibition building, a wall of reflective glass marches relentlessly down an 800-foot (244-meter) long block.

Facetlike indentations give an organizing rhythm to the facade. The viewer's eye slides along, hesitating at each jewel-like edge, breaking the facade into smaller, more comprehensible and interesting sections.

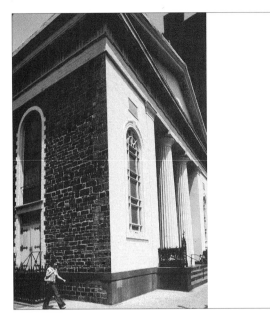

Traditionally, architects have distinguished between the fronts and the sides of buildings. One approach was to make the front fancy (for example, light-colored stucco imitating masonry) and the sides less important (rough-hewn stone, in this case). The result here is a front that looks as though it might easily peel off.

Quoins at the corner securely hook the front to the side, like grasping fingers, suggesting a mechanical connection between the two materials and the two facades.

Quoins grasp like the fingers in this sculpture.

Corners

Like a massive Egyptian step-pyramid, this office building reads as a single mass that has been carved away. It is a closed form, almost forbidding.

Cutting away the corner breaks up the mass. Instead of a single blocky volume, the building begins to appear as an inner volume wrapped in an outer layer.

A layered form (top) and a building with its skin removed emphasize surface rather than volume.

This office building does nothing to mark or celebrate the corner on which it stands.

Adding an extra story at the corner gives the building some visual weight; the emphasis provides an anchor, a kind of exclamation point that draws the eye.

The corner entrance of this small office building juts out like a spear aimed at passers-by, hardly a welcoming gesture.

Carving the corner into a curve disarms it. It is no longer aggressive, but welcoming. The curve even changes the viewer's perception of the material—instead of solid masonry, it seems soft, like cheese.

A column "pressed" into a masonry wall (top) offers another way to suggest softness. The cantilevered corner below might prompt passers-by to move away before it falls.

The block wall left of the gate provides a screen for the space behind but moves aggressively towards the entrance.

Painting a bite out of the wall makes it less aggressive and also offers a bonus. The neobaroque flourish suggests that the wall is deferring, pulling back in a curtsey from the modest entrance.

Deferential curtsey.

This vertical corner is structurally sound, of course, but it doesn't offer any visual emphasis to the sense of support.

Reinforcing the corner with a battered wall (actually a sloping section of offices) creates a more graphic suggestion of support.

Diagonals are bracing.

This corner overlooks a town square of some importance, but the corner doesn't suggest anything of that importance.

A small accent gives the corner additional stature.

Brooch on décolletage.

The sense of surface dominates a prism-shaped office building.

Pressing grooves into the top corners defines a "top" and emphasizes volume as opposed to surface.

Edges

A simple, uncomplicated molding edges an office building entrance with a slight setback at the frame of the opening.

With a modest decorative treatment the edge becomes somewhat more interesting.

An elaborate door edge treatment.

Elements of the facade composition are delineated, separated, and relatively isolated, almost stacked on one another.

Overlapping the separate elements suggests a mechanical link connecting them.

A rather conventional overhang, in the builder's Gothic tradition, protects the side entrance to a house.

Saw-toothed edge adds some visual spice.

These edges bite into the space they define.

The sides of the center tower are like blinders on a horse, forcing the strip windows to face front. One visual consequence is that the building's surface—the planes of its facade—is emphasized, rather than its volume.

Connecting the two facade planes by wrapping the windows around the corner cuts into the confining sides and begins to outline the volume of the space inside.

This tower meets the sky in a simple, Art Deco step-back-and-spire.

Modern gargoyles modeled on Chrysler automobile hood ornaments create a more aggressive silhouette, breaking up the edge and grabbing the sky like claws.

Compare the minimalist approach to meeting the sky (top) with the close-up of the gargoyles reaching out.

Meeting the Ground

A rounded molding tops the base of this apartment house. The stiff, rectilinear articulation below it gives a strong yet relatively static feeling.

When the same articulation is scalloped, its curved shadows suggest lively movement.

A typical modern apartment has a simple, relatively heavy base.

Punching ventilation openings in the plane lightens the meeting of base and ground.

A commercial building is marked by a solid corner.

Deeply cut rustication makes the corner more dramatic, more muscular.

The long, low house is tethered to the earth by a series of thick columns.

Replacing columns with cantilever makes the house float above a shadowed base.

The basement windows of this administration building sit on a separate, solid base.

Cutting the basement windows into the base connects the upper and lower parts of the building and literally eats away at the mass of the base.

Meeting the Sky

The top of the building on the right is compact and closed. It pulls back rather than reaching out and engaging its surroundings.

Punch holes in the structural supports and they capture bits of space, suggesting openness and airiness.

An open loggia captures great hunks of sky.

The top floor of this museum is open to the front like a traditional loggia, but its low ceiling makes it dark and cavelike, a severe edge where the building meets the sky.

Punching holes in the roof lightens the dark underhang and relieves the hard edge of the building.

The crowning sphere of the Viennese Secession building is like a weight holding it down.

Perforating the sphere dissolves it without diminishing its ceremonial role in marking the entrance.

Like most modern slab towers—the you-get-what-you-see school of office tower design—this one just stops at the top.

A comblike crown at the top here gracefully feathers the edge into the sky.

Detail of top.

This straight wall is a barrier, blocking out what is behind it.

The swooping wall announces the dome behind. It's like pulling back a curtain.

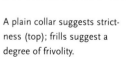

The rigid, taut line of the entrance pediment of this island home suggests formality and stiffness.

With a scalloped edge, the pediment meets the sky with a more frivolous kind of formality.

A plain collar suggests strictness (top); frills suggest a degree of frivolity.

The thick trunk of this apartment tower is overlaid by linear textures created by the patterns of balconies and windows. The balconies, breaking the edge, help dissolve the mass of the trunk and give the impression of tall tower made up of many smaller pieces rather than one huge mass. The top remains a solid cap.

Adding a vertical linear motif at the top contrasts with the horizontals below and presents a more delicate conclusion.

This top continues the general horizontality of the tower shaft.

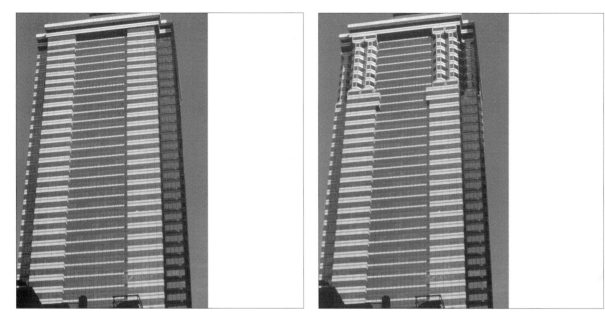

There is a suggestion of an "ending" at the top of this sky-scraper but it is insubstantial—even inconsequential—given the size of the tower.

Molding the top seven floors of offices into colossal double columns at each corner continues the general pattern of the floors below but creates a monumental top.

The bland plane of this roof contrasts starkly with the delicate textures of the facade below and the pinnacle above.

Giving the roof a ribbed copper finish, and adding dormer windows, creates a smoother segue, in terms of visual texture, between the elements above and below.

The texture of this roof occupies the eye and distracts attention from the plane on which it sits.

Perfect symmetry suggests stasis. This Gothic cathedral facade is vertical and forceful in the way it confronts us, but it sits there quietly, with no sense of potential for action, a passive, point-to-heaven approach.

The imbalance of an almost symmetrical facade creates visual tension. The viewer's eye shifts back and forth between the similar-but-different towers, as though waiting for the thrust that will make them equal. These towers are dynamic pointers.

Another kind of tension—unintentionally off the vertical.

A building with a flat top simply stops.

With a kind of crenellation, the building carries a crown in keeping with its rich Venetian Renaissance facade.

A crown (top) and a contemporary architectural version of the crown.

This inverted shape is a protective and comforting form that could house almost any gathering.

The spire is the almost required addition that signifies "church." It makes a perfect foil to the inward-focused shelter by soaring towards the heavens.

The edge of this famous colonnade presents a relatively stern, unrelieved silhouette.

Topping the colonnade with statues softens its edge.

Spires with small spirettes to break up its silhouette.

The same spires are more formally attired, with bejeweled accents that highlight their delicacy.

Detail of spires.

Large-scale detail breaks up the edge of a building top as it meets the sky.

Smaller-scale detail create a finer feathering of the edge, which also holds visual interest at closer range.

This library addition has a rather stark roofline. The inverted Vs of the peaked roofs are containing, sheltering forms. They seem to push down rather than point up.

Breaking the roof silhouettes with ornaments at their highest points punctures the containing forms and reverses their apparent visual direction. Now they are like arrows pointing up.

An inverted "V," a containing form.

These office towers are direct and straightforward, typical examples of the modern, office tower box.

The unique spire gives the tower a conclusion, finishing it off in a way that satisfies expectations that grow from familiarity with towers through the history of architecture. The tapered top also distracts from the bulk of the trunk beneath, feathering it away.

Openings

A canopy shields an entrance from inclement weather but also places it in deep shadow.

Replacing the solid panels with glass dissolves the canopy but still protects against the rain.

Canopies.

The traditional symmetry of buildings creates visual expectations, conscious and unconscious. For example, we expect that the doorway, rose window, and bell tower of this tiny chapel should line up.

When these elements don't line up, a modest but tangible tension results.

Modern teapot with off-center handle and fill-up opening.

A relatively plain, simple entrance for a home.

Lacy ornament celebrates the Victorian entrance and amuses the eye.

A straightforward, serviceable entrance is marked off by columns.

Capping the main opening with an arch emphasizes it and makes it more congenial and welcoming.

A gesture of greeting.

This doorway is wide enough for easy entry, and the window above provides lighting to the interior.

The doorway is no wider here, but the addition of sidelights frames the entrance and makes it more important.

A fancy collar frames the face.

This commercial building has a big, tall entrance, but one that lacks grandeur.

The entrance becomes quite grand when it is overlaid by a ziggurat.

Ziggurat motif as entrance to socialist housing complex.

The main entrance to a large housing complex is quite plain: the designer appears to have just sliced through the building to give access to the courtyard within.

Adding another floor, with tall heralding flagpoles on each side, highlights the opening. Edging the corners with open balconies produces a distinctive visual texture that emphasizes the entrance.

Men with halberds flank an important person.

This townhouse entrance is relatively modest because it is constrained, held down, by the course of soldier bricks (set on their ends) that mark the upper boundary of the lower story.

Topping the doorway with a pediment gives it prominence because it breaks through the constraining soldier course. By violating that boundary the pediment announces that the entrance is the most important feature of the facade.

Emphasized entrances.

A hole cut in a wall offers a modest entrance to this house

A simple arched molding marks the cutout entrance as important. The setback slot slicing through the curve gives additional emphasis.

Same idea—emphasizing the entrance—but a fancier implementation.

The heavy rustication between the windows at the base of this building helps create a sense of monumentality. The windows punch through the base and provide a counterpoint of void vs. solid.

Letting the rustication encroach on the window openings establishes the dominance of mass over void. The windows don't cut through so much as peek from behind the rustication.

Pilasters and a broken pediment enhance the entrance to this charming parish church.

A coat of whitewash is like floodlighting the entrance.

White shirt as contrast with black dinner jacket.

This arrangement of windows gives equal visual weight to each floor.

Pushing the pilasters through the horizontal spandrels creates three-story-high bays and a more monumental facade. The floors are still expressed, but the result is a much grander scale.

This sedate facade is composed of repeated, independent elements. It is static and nondirectional.

Using moldings and string courses to tie the elements together emphasizes the horizontal. The zig–zagging string courses also impart a sense of liveliness and animation.

This solid, semi-traditional house (Cape Cod shingle minus decorative trim) has a stolid but straightforward facade.

Letting the openings slice through the supports at the left maintains the basic form but the asymmetry suggests something dynamic.

The window placement makes the side of this building seem relatively static. The sloped roofline to the right reinforces this quality, suggesting fixed bracing.

Connecting the windows confers directionality and suggests movement, particularly where they break through the corner of the building. The tension created by asymmetrical window placement contributes to this effect. Curving the wall at the right exchanges the "bracing" feeling for one of springy resiliency, also sympathetic to a sense of movement.

Suggestion of movement.

Structure

This university engineering building rests on an arcade of giant piers with outstretched arms. The colonnade implies movement, drawing the eye along a path.

Removing a small segment of the arcade—where the "arms" touch—interrupts the continuity, creating a sequence of discrete, static "T" elements.

The thin structural elements of this famous tower suggest airiness, but the openings at the lower edge have a certain coarseness.

Introducing successive subdivisions softens the edges of the larger openings and suggests greater refinement.

The fine, linear tile ornament on this Persian dome (top) contradicts and disguises its massiveness.

This colossally thick wall provides excellent thermal insulation and structural solidity.

Inserting a narrow, decorative panel does not affect the thermal and structural qualities but diminishes the apparent mass and distracts from the thickness of the wall.

The banding of these arches breaks up their mass.

The underside of this central staircase is ponderous. The sheer thickness of the central, supporting member makes the viewer aware of the tons of concrete that went into it.

Lines in a form almost always reduce its apparent mass. Here the lighted groove in the central, supporting member distracts from its massiveness.

This facade is complex and busy, but also rather static, divided into cubbyholes by the clear, precise horizontals and verticals.

Adding diagonal bracing has several effects: Its narrowness implies transparency and airiness; it is like a net stretched over the facade. The diagonal braces also suggest the tautness of cables in tension and therefore dynamism, imminent movement—reinforced by the diagonal staircase.

This squat, massive column is the epitome of structural solidity.

Adding a vertical molding makes the column seem thinner by dividing the shaft into five separate elements. It also accentuates the column's height, further distracting from its bulk.

Another way to reduce the apparent size of a large element is to paint a mural which takes attention away from its mass.

These tall windows are separated by tall columns.

Adding an ornamental texture to half of the column reduces its apparent height, breaking a tall element into two shorter ones.

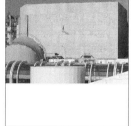

The side of this column is a bland and plain, undecorated surface.

A modest pattern of rivets (side and front) gives visual interest to the surface.

A single element, rather than a pattern, can also distract from a bland surface.

Massive, monolithic column bases support monumental columns.

Incising a groove suggests that the columns and bases aren't monolithic, but are composed of panels placed edge to edge, like a house of cards.

The thinness of scored cardboard.

SCORE & BEND

The very heftiness of this pier suggests it is supporting a great weight.

If thickness suggests mass, slenderness suggests delicacy and lightness. Tapering the supporting pier makes a delicate visual point—that the weight supported cannot be so great.

A modest support suggests that the object being held up isn't so heavy.

The main artery of this university building channels student traffic to destinations such as the coffee shop and campus store. It serves its utilitarian purpose as a people conduit.

A few wisps of neon transform an industrial-strength corridor into a ceremonial avenue. The viewer's eye supplies the continuity between the neon vaults, while the mind fills in the historical associations.

An historical reference: the nave of St. Peter's, Rome.

This long low building doesn't look as long and low as it might—it is only two stories high and runs a full city block. The columns that cut through the first floor cornice interrupt the sweep of our eye.

Letting the cornice shoot past the columns removes the visual obstructions.

Detail of column cutting through cornice.

Broad, stocky piers and a wafer-thin roof sliver look mismatched. The over-scaled piers seem inappropriate given the apparent lightness of what they're carrying.

When the piers and roof are separated by a little cushion—a slender beam—the roof seems suspended, floating above the piers. The contrast between fat and slender remains, but the breathing room between removes the apparent discrepancy.

This monumental facade is composed of two powerful horizontal layers separated by a heavy first floor cornice.

Pushing the pilasters through the cornice breaks the dominant horizontality and creates a two-story order that unites the two layers of the building.

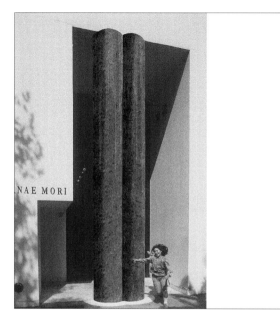

The solid, double-column motif in granite dramatically divides the in and out traffic to and from this retail store.

The traffic remains divided, but reflective chrome cladding effectively dissolves the columns, and the huge cylinders lose much of their weight and obtrusiveness.

Details

The brackets have a fresh, robust curve, but are rather blocky and crude.

An incised line reinforces the curve of the forms but also reduces their apparent bulk, because the eye follows the line rather than the plane into which it is cut.

This formidable staircase leads to a modest home.

Applying colors (black stairs, red railing tops, pink and aqua inside and outside of the railing) encourages the eye to flit from one part to another, and distracts from its massiveness.

This mural of painted pedestrians also distracts our attention from the solidity of the wall, but by interesting us in its subject matter.

These pilaster-like panels end with a simple block. It is rather severe and graceless.

A simple, delicate crimping gives the top a decorative emphasis and creates an "ending" to the element.

Thick mullions and window trim look rather heavy-handed.

Adding a shadow line lightens the mullions, subdividing the horizontals and verticals into thinner and visually lighter elements.

Multiple moldings provide lines that lighten an interior cornice of a Bavarian church .

Except for the pilasters' ornamental topping, the severe shadows and the unadorned windows present a somewhat plain, lackluster facade.

Detailing the window surrounds with dentil courses and moldings creates a richer facade texture.

The base and upper stories of this building are barely connected, separated by an entablature-like neutral zone. It looks as though the top could slide off the bottom with little resistance.

Bringing the upper-story mullions down into the neutral zone and clamping them there creates a visual connection—they are woven together. The dark, narrow columns of the upper facade are captured in the same way.

Detail of connecting mullions.

Travelers routinely face seemingly endless airline terminal corridors like this one.

A single neon strip spanning the corridor with a tilting, off-balance line offers an abstract but persuasive suggestion of the human gait. It also interrupts the eye's progress down the corridor, effectively dividing the long tunnel into two shorter sections.

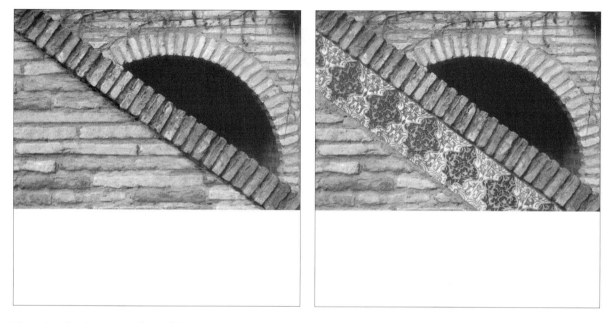

The railing for the stairway beyond has a simple cap of bricks laid on their edges.

Adding a border of decorative tile below the railing visually dissolves the brick wall. Because the patterned tile doesn't suggest support, as the bricks do, the upper portion of the railing seems to float.

This massive wall forms a flat, solid backdrop to a university common room.

A mural breaks up the wall with forms that distract our eye from its flat surface.

The same principle applied to a sinuous vase: a realistic landscape view destroys its solid form.

This narrow urban interior could inspire claustrophobia. The granite walls threaten to squeeze in.

The mirror is a hallowed device of interior architecture. They are solid objects, but their reflections deny that solidity. The wall dissolves and expands, creating a double-wide space.

Reflection dissolving a wall.

The boxy volumes of the elevator enclosures dominate this office building lobby.

Two visual devices reduce the apparent bulk of the enclosures. Ornamental lines, thin (above) and fat (below), divide the blocks into upper and lower sections. The varying line weights also suggest relative importance: the pinstriped upper section is intended as background; the bolder stripes below suggest a monumental modern rusticated base.

Credits

CREDITS

Book page	Element	Building	City	State	Country	Architect	Style	Dates
10	Facade	Exchange Place Centre	Jersey City	NJ	US	Grad Associates	Modern	1989
11	Facade	House	Sag Harbor	NY	US	Unknown	Colonial	
12	Facade	Washington Square Hotel	New York	NY	US	Unknown	Revival	
13	Facade	Townhouse	Brooklyn	NY	US	Unknown	Revival	
14	Facade	School	Delft		Netherlands	Unknown	Revival	
15	Facade	John Hancock Center	Chicago	IL	US	Skidmore, Owings & Merrill	Modern	1969
16	Facade	New Britain Township Building	New Britain	PA	US	George J. Donovan & Associates	Modern	1990
17	Facade	Condé Nast Building	New York	NY	US	Fox & Fowle Architects	Modern	2000
18	Facade	Office building	New York	NY	US	Unknown	Modern	
19	Facade	W. R. Grace Building	New York	NY	US	Skidmore, Owings & Merrill	Modern	1974
20	Facade	Miele Headquarters	Princeton	NJ	US	Michael Graves	Postmodern	1999
21	Facade	Center for Jewish Life	Princeton	NJ	US	Robert A. M. Stern Architects	Postmodern	1993
22	Facade	Forum des Halles	Paris		France	Unknown	Modern	1979
23	Facade	Guild House	Philadelphia	PA	US	Venturi and Rauch	Postmodern	1965
24	Facade	Townhouses	New York	NY	US	Unknown	Folk	
25	Facade	Upper West Side apartment building	New York	NY	US	Unknown	Modern	
26	Facade	St. Theresa's Roman Catholic Cathedral	Hamilton		Bermuda	Unknown	Revival	
27	Facade	Judson Memorial Church	New York	NY	US	McKim, Mead & White	Revival	1892
28	Facade	John Hancock Tower	Boston	MA	US	I. M. Pei & Partners	Modern	1973
29	Facade	St. Peter's Basilica	Rome		Italy	Carlo Maderno	Renaissance	1614 (facade)
30	Facade	Councilor's Tavern	Rothenburg ob der Tauber		Germany	Unknown	Renaissance	1446

Book page	Element	Building	City	State	Country	Architect	Style	Dates
31	Facade	Doge's Palace	Venice		Italy	Unknown	Gothic	12th–15th centuries
32	Facade	Majolica House	Vienna		Austria	Otto Wagner	Art Nouveau	1898–99
33	Facade	Forum des Halles	Paris		France	Unknown	Modern	1986
34	Facade	Olbrich House	Darmstadt		Germany	Josef Maria Olbrich	Modern	1901
35	Facade	Weinberg Terrace	Pittsburgh	PA	US	J. David Hoglund, Perkins Eastmen Architects	Postmodern	1997
36	Facade	Museum of Modern Art apartments	New York	NY	US	Caesar Pelli	Modern	1984
37	Facade	Solow Building	New York	NY	US	Skidmore, Owings & Merrill	Modern	1973
38	Facade	World Financial Center	New York	NY	US	Caesar Pelli	Modern	
39	Facade	Brazilian Pavilion, City University of Paris	Paris		France	Le Corbusier	Modern	1959
40	Facade	Schullin's Jewelry Shop	Vienna		Austria	Hans Hollein	Modern	1974
41	Facade	House	Savannah	GA	US	Unknown	Revival	
42	Facade	Washington Court	New York	NY	US	James Stewart Polshek & Partners	Postmodern	1986
43	Facade	Basilica	Vicenza		Italy	Andrea Palladio	Renaissance	1548–1617
44	Facade	Apartment building	New York	NY	US	Unknown	Art Deco	
45	Facade	Harborside Financial Center	Jersey City	NJ	US	Beyer Blinder Belle	Modern	1990
46	Facade	IBM Building (now Verizon)	Fort Wayne	IN	US	Skidmore, Owings & Merrill	Modern	1969
47	Facade	Fire Headquarters	New Haven	CT	US	Peter Millard	Modern	1961
48	Facade	Office building	New York	NY	US	Unknown	Eclectic	
49	Facade	Plaza de Toros de la Maestranza	Seville		Spain	Juan Talavera 1881; Aníbal González 1915	Baroque	19th–20th centuries
50	Facade	Commercial building	Village near Oaxaca		Mexico	Unknown	Folk	

CREDITS

Book page	Element	Building	City	State	Country	Architect	Style	Dates
51	Facade	Whitehead Campus Center	Haverford	PA	US	Dagit-Saylor Architects	Postmodern	1993
52	Facade	Brazilian Pavilion, City University	Paris		France	Le Corbusier	Modern	1953
53	Facade	J. K. Javits Center	New York	NY	US	James Ingo Freed of I. M. Pei & Partners	Modern	1986
54	Facade	St. Joseph's Roman Catholic Church	New York	NY	US	John Doran	Revival	1834
56	Corner	World Financial Center	New York	NY	US	Caesar Pelli	Modern	1986
57	Corner	Office building	Rotterdam		Netherlands	Unknown	Modern	
58	Corner	Commercial building (Resort Properties, Ltd.)	Westhampton Beach	NY	US	Unknown	Eclectic	
59	Corner	Housing	Delft		Netherlands	Unknown	Modern	
60	Corner	Originally Westyard Distribution Center	New York	NY	US	Davis Brody & Associates	Modern	1970
61	Corner	NW corner of piazzetta off of Zócalo	Oaxaca		Mexico	Unknown	Folk	
62	Corner	The Continental Center	New York	NY	US	Der Scutt	Modern	1983
64	Edge	Office building	New York	NY	US	Unknown	Revival	
65	Edge	World Wide Plaza	New York	NY	US	Skidmore, Owings & Merrill, David Childs, Design Partner	Modern	1989
66	Edge	House	New Hope	PA	US	Unknown	Folk	
67	Edge	Office building	New York	NY	US	Unknown	Modern	
68	Edge	Chrysler Building	New York	NY	US	William Van Alen	Art Deco	1930
70	Meeting the Ground	Apartment building	New York	NY	US	Hardy Holzman Pfeiffer Associates	Postmodern	

Book page	Element	Building	City	State	Country	Architect	Style	Dates
71	Meeting the Ground	University Village	New York	NY	US	I. M. Pei & Partners	Modern	1970
72	Meeting the Ground	Guardian Life Insurance Co.	New York	NY	US	D'Oench & Yost	Revival	1911
73	Meeting the Ground	Elevated house	Bridgehampton	NY	US	Unknown	Modern	
74	Meeting the Ground	Administration, Brown University	Providence	RI	US	Unknown	Eclectic	
76	Meeting the Sky	I. Magnin	Chicago	IL	US	Unknown	Modern	
77	Meeting the Sky	Museum of Modern Art	New York	NY	US	Philip Goodwin and Edward Durrell Stone	Modern	1939
78	Meeting the Sky	Secession House	Vienna		Austria	Josef Maria Olbrich	Modern	1896
79	Meeting the Sky	Carnegie Hall Tower	New York	NY	US	Caesar Pelli & Associates	Modern	1990
80	Meeting the Sky	United Nations General Assembly	New York	NY	US	Wallace K. Harrison	Modern	1953
81	Meeting the Sky	Brant House	Hamilton		Bermuda	Venturi & Rauch	Postmodern	1977
82	Meeting the Sky	Trump Palace	New York	NY	US	Frank Williams & Associates Architects	Postmodern	1991
83	Meeting the Sky	Morgan Guaranty Building	New York	NY	US	Kevin Roche, John Dinkeloo & Associates	Postmodern	1988
84	Meeting the Sky	Office building	New York	NY	US	H. Craig Severance and Yasuo Matsui	Revival	1929
85	Meeting the Sky	Chartres Cathedral	Chartres		France	Unknown	Gothic	1194–1260

CREDITS

Book page	Element	Building	City	State	Country	Architect	Style	Dates
86	Meeting the Sky	Procuratie Vecchia	Venice		Italy	Unknown	Renaissance	Early 16th century
87	Meeting the Sky	North Christian Church	Columbus	IN	US	Eero Saarinen	Modern	1964
88	Meeting the Sky	Colonnade of St. Peter's	Rome		Italy	Gian Lorenzo Bernini	Renaissance	1656 to 1667
89	Meeting the Sky	Tyn Church	Prague		Czech Republic	Unknown	Gothic	1350–1511
90	Meeting the Sky	St. Mark's	Venice		Italy	Unknown	Gothic	1063–1073
91	Meeting the Sky	East Hampton Library	East Hampton	NY	US	Robert A. M. Stern Architects	Postmodern	1997
92	Meeting the Sky	Chrysler Building	New York	NY	US	William Van Alen	Art Deco	1930
94	Openings	Washington Court	New York	NY	US	James Stewart Polshek & Partners	Modern	1986
95	Openings	Chapel	Val d'Aosta		Italy	Unknown	Folk	
96	Openings	House	Sag Harbor	NY	US	Unknown	Victorian	
97	Openings	Princeton University Computer Science Building	Princeton	NJ	US	R.M. Klim Jennifer M. Greene, Associates & Frances Halsband Architects	Postmodern	1989
98	Openings	House	Delft		Netherlands	Unknown	Folk	
99	Openings	575 Fifth Avenue	New York	NY	US	Emery Roth & Sons	Postmodern	1985
100	Openings	Friedrich Engels Hof at Brigittenau	Vienna		Austria	Rudolf Perco	Art Deco	1930–33
101	Openings	Apartment	New York	NY	US	Unknown	Revival	
102	Openings	Vanna Venturi House	Chestnut Hill	PA	US	Venturi and Rauch	Postmodern	1962

Book page	Element	Building	City	State	Country	Architect	Style	Dates
103	Openings	United States Customs House	New York	NY	US	Cass Gilbert	Revival	1902–1907
104	Openings	San José	Oaxaca		Mexico	Unknown	Baroque	
105	Openings	Puck Building	New York	NY	US	Albert Wagner	Revival	1886
106	Openings	Office building	New York	NY	US	Unknown	Eclectic	
107	Openings	House	Bridgehampton	NY	US	Unknown	Modern	
108	Openings	Asphalt Green Aqua Center	New York	NY	US	Richard Dattner	Modern	1993
110	Structure	Becton Center (Becton Davies)	New Haven	CT	US	Marcel Breuer	Modern	1970
111	Structure	Eiffel Tower	Paris		France	Gustav Eiffel	Technical	1889
112	Structure	Caravan Seri	Shiraz		Iran	Unknown	Mogul	
113	Structure	Whitehead Campus Center	Haverford	PA	US	Dagit-Saylor Architects	Modern	1993
114	Structure	Pompidou Centre	Paris		France	Renzo Piano and Richard Rogers	Modern	1986
115	Structure	Hotel	Oaxaca		Mexico	Unknown	Revival	
116	Structure	Unity Temple	Oak Park	IL	US	Frank Lloyd Wright	Modern	1906
117	Structure	Postal Savings Bank	Vienna		Austria	Otto Wagner	Modern	1906
118	Structure	Morgan Guaranty Building	New York	NY	US	Kevin Roche, John Dinkeloo & Associates	Modern	1988
119	Structure	Beineke Rare Book Library	New Haven	CT	US	Skidmore, Owings & Merrill	Modern	1963
120	Structure	Trabant University Center	Newark	DE	US	Venturi, Scott Brown & Associates	Modern	1996
121	Structure	Warehouse	New York	NY	US	Unknown	Eclectic	
122	Structure	Columbus Post Office	Columbus	IN	US	Kevin Roche, John Dinkeloo & Associates	Modern	1970
123	Structure	Capitoline Museum (Palazzo Nuovo)	Rome		Italy	Michelangelo	Renaissance	1603–1654
124	Structure	Hanae Mori Store	New York	NY	US	Hans Hollein	Modern	1969

CREDITS

Book page	Element	Building	City	State	Country	Architect	Style	Dates
126	Details	House	Sag Harbor	NY	US	Unknown	Revival	
127	Details	House	Browns Town		Jamaica	Unknown	Folk	
128	Details	Rockefeller Center	New York	NY	US	Raymond Hood, Godley & Fouilhoux	Art Deco	1940
129	Details	Seagram Building	New York	NY	US	Mies van der Rohe with Philip Johnson, Design Architects	Modern	1958
130	Details	Office building	New York	NY	US	Unknown	Revival	
131	Details	565 Fifth Avenue	New York	NY	US	Norman Jaffe	Modern	1993
132	Details	Schiphol Airport	Amsterdam		Netherlands	Unknown	Modern	
133	Details	Restaurant	Cordoba		Spain	Unknown	Folk	
134	Details	Swiss Pavilion, City University of Paris	Paris		France	Le Corbusier and Lúcio Costa	Modern	1959
135	Details	Bank (destroyed)	New York	NY	US	Unknown	Modern	
136	Details	Film Center Building	New York	NY	US	Buchman & Kahn	Art Deco	1929